MW01200606

# MOVIE TRIOS FOR ALL

## Playable on ANY THREE INSTRUMENTS
## or any number of instruments in ensemble

**Arranged by Michael Story**

Alfred

ISBN-10: 0-7390-6319-7
ISBN-13: 978-0-7390-6319-4

# BELIEVE
## (From "The Polar Express" - 2004)

Bb TRUMPET/BARITONE T.C.

Words and Music by
ALAN SILVESTRI and GLEN BALLARD
*Arranged by MICHAEL STORY*

# AS TIME GOES BY
## (From "Casablanca" - 1942)

Words and Music by
HERMAN HUPFELD
*Arranged by MICHAEL STORY*

33530

# CAN'T FIGHT THE MOONLIGHT
## (From "Coyote Ugly" - 2000)

Words and Music by
DIANE WARREN
*Arranged by MICHAEL STORY*

# HOW THE WEST WAS WON
## Main Title
### (From "How the West Was Won" - 1962)

Music by ALFRED NEWMAN
Lyrics by KEN DARBY
*Arranged by MICHAEL STORY*

D.C. al Coda        $\oplus$ *Coda*

# IF I ONLY HAD A BRAIN
## (From "The Wizard of Oz" - 1939)

Music by HAROLD ARLEN
Lyrics by E.Y. HARBURG
*Arranged by MICHAEL STORY*

D.S. 𝄋 al Coda          𝄌 Coda

# NIMBUS 2000
## (From "Harry Potter and the Sorcerer's Stone" - 2001)

Music by **JOHN WILLIAMS**
*Arranged by MICHAEL STORY*

# YOU'VE GOT A FRIEND IN ME
## (From "Toy Story" - 1995)

Words and Music by
RANDY NEWMAN
*Arranged by* MICHAEL STORY

33530

# MAMMA MIA
## (From "Mamma Mia!" - 2008)

Words and Music by BENNY ANDERSSON,
STIG ANDERSON and BJORN ULVAEUS
*Arranged by MICHAEL STORY*

# BATMAN THEME
## (From "Batman" - 1989)

By DANNY ELFMAN
*Arranged by MICHAEL STORY*

# CANTINA BAND
## (From "Star Wars" - 1977)

Music by **JOHN WILLIAMS**
*Arranged by MICHAEL STORY*

# IMPERIAL MARCH
## "Darth Vader's Theme"
### (From "Star Wars: The Empire Strikes Back" - 1980)

Music by **JOHN WILLIAMS**
*Arranged by MICHAEL STORY*

# JAMES BOND THEME
## (From the James Bond Series – 1962-2008)

By MONTY NORMAN
*Arranged by MICHAEL STORY*

# THEME FROM "ICE CASTLES"
## (Through the Eyes of Love)
### (From "Ice Castles" - 1978)

Music by MARVIN HAMLISCH
Lyrics by CAROLE BAYER SAGER
*Arranged by MICHAEL STORY*

# YOU'RE THE ONE THAT I WANT
## (From "Grease" - 1978)

Words and Music by
JOHN FARRAR
*Arranged by MICHAEL STORY*

**Moderately fast**

# RAIDERS MARCH
## (From "Raiders of the Lost Ark" - 1981)

Music by **JOHN WILLIAMS**
*Arranged by MICHAEL STORY*